BE YOUR OWN BOSS.

"The Ultimate Guide to Starting a Business as a Teenager,"

BY

CAROL SICHEMBO.

BOOK OUTLINE.

Introduction.

Why be your own boss? (Benefits of entrepreneurship for teenagers - independence, learning, income)

Who is this ebook for? (Identifying the target audience and their needs)

What you'll learn in this guide (Overview of the ebook structure)

II. Finding Your Business Idea.

Brainstorming: Identifying your passions, skills, and interests

Market research: Understanding your target audience and their needs

Validating your idea: Testing the feasibility and potential of your business

Popular business ideas for teenagers (Examples across different categories)

Choosing the right business for you (Factors to consider: scalability, startup costs, personal fit)

III. Planning for Success

Setting SMART goals (Specific, Measurable, Achievable, Relevant, Time-bound)

Writing a business plan (Simplified overview for teenagers)

Legal considerations for young entrepreneurs (Permits, licenses, regulations)

Financing your business (Creative options for teenagers - bootstrapping, crowdfunding)

Time management for busy teens (Strategies for balancing school, work, and personal life)

IV. Launching Your Business

Branding your business (Creating a name, logo, and online presence)

Marketing on a budget (Social media marketing, local advertising, word-of-mouth)

Building a strong customer base (Strategies for attracting and retaining customers)

Pricing your products or services (Setting competitive prices and considering profit margins)

V. Running Your Business Like a Pro

Customer service: Building positive relationships with clients

Recordkeeping and basic accounting (Tracking income and expenses)

Dealing with challenges and setbacks (Problem-solving and overcoming obstacles)

The power of positive thinking: Maintaining a growth mindset

VI. Growing Your Business

Expanding your product or service offerings

Building a team: Hiring and working with other teenagers (if applicable)

Taking your business online (E-commerce options for digital products or services)

Reaching new markets (Expanding your customer base beyond your local area)

VII. Conclusion

Recap.

Final words of encouragement.

Introduction: Be Your Own Boss - Unleashing Your Inner Entrepreneur

Have you ever dreamt of being your own boss? Imagine calling the shots, setting your own hours, and seeing the fruits of your labor blossom into a thriving business. For many teenagers, this might seem like a distant dream, a reality reserved for adults in suits and ties. But what if we told you that entrepreneurship isn't just for grown-ups? That with the right guidance, passion, and a dash of hustle, you, as a teenager, can be the architect of your own success story?

This book, "Be Your Own Boss: The Ultimate Guide to Starting a Business as a Teenager," is your roadmap to turning that entrepreneurial dream into a tangible reality. We understand the unique challenges and opportunities that teenagers face. You're brimming with fresh ideas, boundless energy, and a willingness to learn. But navigating the world of business can seem daunting, especially when juggling school, extracurricular activities, and the ever-present pull of social life.

Why Be Your Own Boss? The Allure of Entrepreneurship

So, why take the plunge and become your own boss? The answer lies in the incredible benefits that entrepreneurship offers teenagers. Here are just a few reasons why starting your own business could be the most empowering adventure you embark on:

- **Be Your Own Decision Maker:** Tired of following someone else's rules? As a business owner, you get to chart your own course. You decide what products or services to offer, how to market them, and how to run your day-to-day operations. This freedom and control are incredibly empowering and allow you to truly express your creativity and vision.
- **Learn Valuable Life Skills:** Running a business is an education in itself. You'll develop essential skills like marketing, finance, customer service, and problem-solving. These skills are valuable not only in the business world but also

in everyday life. The confidence and know-how you gain will equip you to tackle any challenge that comes your way.
- **Turn Your Passion into Profit:** Do you have a hobby you absolutely love? What if you could turn that passion into a source of income? Whether it's baking delicious cookies, writing captivating stories, or creating stunning artwork, entrepreneurship allows you to monetize your talents and share them with the world.
- **Be Your Own Success Story:** Imagine the satisfaction of building something from the ground up. Seeing your business grow and thrive, knowing that your hard work and dedication are paying off, is an incredibly rewarding experience.

This book is for any teenager who harbors a spark of entrepreneurial spirit. Whether you're a budding artist with creations to share or a tech whiz with digital solutions to offer, this guide is here to equip you with the knowledge and tools you need to launch your dream business. We understand that everyone's entrepreneurial journey is unique. Perhaps you have a fully formed business idea in mind, or maybe you're simply curious about the possibilities. This ebook caters to both. We'll guide you through the process of brainstorming ideas, validating their potential, and finally, turning them into thriving ventures.

What You'll Learn in This Guide

This comprehensive guide is designed to be your one-stop shop for everything you need to know about starting a business as a teenager. Here's a sneak peek at what awaits you in the following chapters:

- **Finding Your Business Idea:** We'll delve into the world of brainstorming, helping you identify your strengths, interests, and the needs of your target audience. We'll also explore popular business ideas that are well-suited for teenagers, offering inspiration and a springboard for your own creative thinking.
- **Planning for Success:** Before diving headfirst into your business venture, we'll guide you through the essential steps of creating a business plan. This simplified plan will help you set clear goals, understand your finances, and establish a roadmap for success. We'll also discuss legal considerations that teenagers need to be aware of and explore creative financing options to get your business off the ground.
- **Launching Your Business:** From crafting a catchy business name and designing a logo to establishing a strong online presence, we'll equip you with the tools to launch your business with style. We'll also teach you effective marketing strategies that don't require a hefty budget, helping you reach your target audience and build a loyal customer base.
- **Running Your Business Like a Pro:** Customer service is the backbone of any successful business, and we'll provide you with tips to build positive relationships with your.

Chapter 2: Finding Your Business Idea - Unearthing the Entrepreneurial Spark Within

Congratulations on taking the first step towards becoming your own boss! The world of entrepreneurship is brimming with possibilities, but the journey begins with a single crucial element: your business idea. This chapter will guide you through the exciting process of brainstorming, identifying hidden opportunities, and ultimately, discovering the perfect business concept that aligns with your passions and skills.

Igniting the Spark: Brainstorming Like a Boss

The first step in finding your business idea is unleashing your inner creative genius. Brainstorming is a powerful tool that allows you to explore a multitude of possibilities and unearth hidden gems. Here are some effective brainstorming techniques:

- **Mind Mapping:** Grab a large piece of paper and write down "Business Idea" in the center. Let your mind wander and jot down any words, phrases, or even doodles that come to mind related to your interests, skills, or problems you encounter in your daily life. Draw lines connecting these ideas to see if patterns or unique combinations emerge.
- **The Power of "What If?":** Challenge yourself to think outside the box. Ask yourself "What if...?" questions related to everyday tasks or problems you observe. For example, "What if I could create a more convenient way to organize my school supplies?" or "What if there was a faster way to learn a new language?" These questions can spark innovative solutions that translate into compelling business ideas.
- **Research and Inspiration:** The world around you is a treasure trove of potential business ideas. Explore online marketplaces like Etsy or local craft fairs to see what products are trending. Read about successful young entrepreneurs and analyze their journeys. Sometimes, the best ideas come from finding a gap in the market or improving upon existing products or services.

From Passion to Profit: Aligning Your Business Idea with Your Strengths

Remember, the ideal business idea isn't just about a cool product or service. It should also tap into your strengths and passions. Here's how to find that sweet spot:

- **What are you good at?** Make a list of your skills and talents. Are you a whiz at computer programming? Do you possess a creative flair for design? Even seemingly everyday skills like baking, writing, or organizing can translate into valuable offerings for your business.
- **What are you passionate about?** What activities make you lose track of time? Do you have a deep love for animals or a fascination with science? Passion fuels motivation and creativity, so consider turning your hobby or interest into a profitable venture.

Finding the Need: Validating Your Business Idea

Once you have a few promising business ideas in mind, the next step is to validate their potential. Here's how to ensure your entrepreneurial venture addresses a real need in the market:

- **Market Research:** Conduct some basic market research to understand your target audience. Who are you trying to sell your product or service to? What are their needs and pain points? Talking to potential customers, conducting online surveys, and analyzing competitor offerings are valuable techniques to assess the market demand for your idea.
- **The Power of Prototyping:** Before investing heavily in your business, consider creating a simple prototype of your product or service. This could be a physical prototype, a basic website design, or even a written proposal outlining your service offering. Testing this prototype with potential customers allows you to

gather valuable feedback and refine your idea before fully launching your business.

Teenage CEOs Who Started Small: Inspiration from Young Pioneers

The world of entrepreneurship is filled with inspiring stories of young people who dared to dream big and turned their ideas into realities. Let's take a closer look at some remarkable teenage CEOs who started small and achieved incredible success:

- **Mikaila Ulmer (Me & The Bees Lemonade):** At just four years old, Mikaila noticed a decline in bee populations near her home. Inspired to help, she created a delicious lemonade recipe using honey from her family's beekeeping business. Mikaila's "Me & The Bees Lemonade" not only offered a refreshing drink but also donated a portion of its proceeds to bee conservation efforts. What started as a small stand at a local farmers market has blossomed into a nationally recognized brand, showcasing the power of passion and social responsibility.
- **Isabella Dymalovski (Luv Ur Skin):** Isabella, at the age of nine, witnessed the struggles her mother faced with sensitive skin. Driven to find a solution, she embarked on a journey to create a natural, chemical-free skincare line. Starting with simple ingredients from her kitchen, Isabella formulated her first product, a lip balm. Through perseverance and dedication, "Luv Ur Skin" has expanded its product line and garnered a loyal following. Isabella's story exemplifies the power of identifying a personal need and turning it into a successful business venture.
- **Evan and Logan Thomas (Mochi Dough):** These twin brothers, at the tender age of 14, discovered a shared passion for Japanese mochi, a soft and chewy rice cake. However, they found it difficult to find high-quality mochi in their local stores. Determined to fill this gap, Evan and Logan started experimenting with recipes in their home kitchen.

Their delicious and innovative mochi flavors, paired with creative marketing strategies, quickly captured the attention of local customers. From a small operation to partnerships with local cafes, Mochi Dough demonstrates the power of identifying a niche market and capitalizing on a unique product offering.

- **Frankie & Mia (Frankie & Mia's Cookies):** This inspiring story highlights the power of sibling collaboration. Frankie, at the age of 11, began baking delicious cookies in his free time. His sister, Mia, who possessed a natural talent for marketing, recognized the potential of his creations. Together, they started "Frankie & Mia's Cookies," selling their homemade treats at local farmers markets. Their vibrant packaging, coupled with the irresistible taste of their cookies, led to a loyal customer base. Frankie & Mia's story proves that even the simplest ideas, when executed with passion and teamwork, can be a recipe for success.
- **Kelvin Doe (SL Educate):** Kelvin Doe's story is a testament to the power of ingenuity and resourcefulness. Growing up in Sierra Leone, a country with limited access to electricity, Kelvin's curiosity about electronics led him to create a battery charger from scrap materials. His innovative designs caught the attention of international media, and Kelvin was offered scholarships to prestigious universities. He ultimately chose to return to Sierra Leone and founded SL Educate, a company that provides affordable educational resources to children in his home country. Kelvin's journey serves as an inspiration to young entrepreneurs who are passionate about using their skills to make a positive impact on the world.

These are just a few examples of the many young people who have taken the entrepreneurial leap. Their stories showcase the potential that lies within each teenager. Remember, your business idea doesn't have to be revolutionary. It can start small, fueled by your passion and a desire to solve a problem or offer a unique product or service.

Now that you've been inspired by these real-life examples, let's delve deeper into the brainstorming process and explore some specific ideas that might spark your own entrepreneurial journey!

Here are some takeaway points.

- **Humor:** Consider adding a touch of humor to keep the chapter engaging. You could include a funny anecdote about a brainstorming session gone wrong or a light-hearted meme related to entrepreneurship.
- **Interactive elements:** Think about incorporating interactive elements like quizzes or worksheets that help readers identify their strengths and interests. This can be a fun way to get them actively involved in the brainstorming process.
- **Visuals:** Break up the text with visuals like infographics or mind maps to illustrate key points and make the chapter more visually appealing for young readers.
- **Case studies:** In addition to the teenage CEO success stories, consider including a brief case study of a teenage business that failed. Analyze what went wrong and use it as a learning opportunity to highlight the importance of market research, financial planning, and adapting to challenges.
- **Beyond Products:** While the chapter focuses on product ideas, consider adding a section on service-based businesses that teenagers can start. This could include anything from pet sitting and tutoring to social media management and graphic design services.
- **Local Focus:** Encourage your readers to think about their local community when brainstorming ideas. Are there any local needs or problems that they could

address with their business? This can be a great way to make a positive impact and tap into a readily available customer base.
- **Environmental Awareness:** Weave in a message about environmental awareness. Discuss ways teenagers can incorporate sustainable practices into their businesses, whether it's using recycled materials or offering eco-friendly products.
- **Global Inspiration:** Don't limit the success stories to just American teenagers. Look for inspiring young entrepreneurs from around the world and showcase their diverse ideas and journeys.

Chapter III: Planning for Success - Building the Blueprint for Your Teenage Empire

Congratulations! You've unearthed a brilliant business idea. Now, it's time to transform that idea from a spark in your mind to a thriving reality. This chapter will equip you with the essential tools for planning your business venture, ensuring it launches with a solid foundation and a clear path to success.

Setting SMART Goals: The Roadmap to Achievement

Every successful business starts with a clear vision and achievable goals. Here's where SMART goals come in. SMART stands for:

- **Specific:** Clearly define what you want to achieve. Instead of a vague goal like "grow my business," aim for something specific like "increase online sales by 20% within the next three months."
- **Measurable:** How will you track your progress? Establish clear metrics to measure your goals. For example, the number of website visitors, social media followers, or units sold.
- **Attainable:** Be realistic about what you can achieve within a given timeframe. Don't set yourself up for discouragement by aiming for the impossible.
- **Relevant:** Ensure your goals align with your overall business vision. Are they relevant to the growth and success of your company?
- **Time-bound:** Set a specific deadline for achieving your goals. This creates a sense of urgency and helps you stay focused.

Crafting a Powerful Business Plan: Your Guidepost to Growth

A business plan might sound intimidating, but for teenagers, it can be a simplified roadmap that guides your entrepreneurial journey. Think of it as a living document that you can refine as your business evolves. Here are the key components of a basic business plan for teenagers:

- **Executive Summary:** A brief overview of your business, including your unique selling proposition (USP) - what makes your product or service stand out?
- **Company Description:** Outline the type of business you are running, the products or services you offer, and your target market.
- **Market Analysis:** Who are your ideal customers? What are their needs and wants? Understanding your target market is crucial for success.
- **Marketing Strategy:** How will you reach your target audience? Explore cost-effective marketing strategies like social media marketing, local advertising, and influencer partnerships.
- **Management Plan:** Who will be responsible for different aspects of the business? Will you be working alone, or do you have a team (friends, family) involved?
- **Financial Projections:** Estimate your startup costs, potential revenue, and projected profits. This helps you understand your financial viability and make informed decisions.

**Don't worry, you don't need a fancy business plan template! Many online resources offer free, easy-to-use templates specifically designed for teenagers.

Legal Considerations for Young Entrepreneurs: Navigating the Rules

As a young entrepreneur, it's important to be aware of basic legal considerations that might apply to your business. Here are some things to keep in mind:

- **Business Permits and Licenses:** Depending on your location and business model, you might need certain permits or licenses to operate legally. Research

local regulations and obtain any necessary licenses before launching your business.
- **Business Structure:** Will you operate as a sole proprietorship, a partnership with a friend, or another legal structure? Understanding the implications of each structure can help you choose the one that best suits your needs.
- **Minors and Business Ownership:** Since you're a teenager, there might be legal limitations related to entering into contracts or handling finances. Consider involving a supportive adult like a parent or guardian to navigate these aspects.

Remember, legal requirements can vary depending on your location. Consulting with a local business advisor or a lawyer specializing in small businesses can provide you with more specific guidance.

Financing Your Teenage Dream: Launching Without Breaking the Bank

Let's face it, most teenagers don't have a hefty sum of money sitting around to invest in a business. But that doesn't have to be a barrier! Here are some creative ways to finance your venture:

- **Bootstrapping:** This involves starting small and reinvesting your profits back into the business to grow it organically. Start with a minimal investment and focus on using resources you already have.
- **Savings and Allowance Power:** Put your savings and allowance to good use! Every dollar saved is a dollar you can invest in your business.
- **Crowdfunding:** Platforms like Kickstarter and GoFundMe allow you to raise funds from a large pool of people online. Create a compelling campaign that showcases your business idea and attracts potential investors.
- **Pre-Sales:** Offer pre-orders for your products or services before you officially launch. This can generate some revenue upfront and help gauge customer interest.

- **Barter System:** Explore the power of bartering! Can you offer your skills or services in exchange for something you need for your business? This could involve trading website design work for marketing materials or offering tutoring in exchange for printing services.
- **Grants and Competitions:** Many organizations offer grants and competitions specifically for young entrepreneurs. Research opportunities in your area and showcase your business idea to win valuable funding.
- **Get Creative with Resources:** Think outside the box! Can you borrow equipment from a friend or family member instead of buying it outright? Utilize free online tools for design, accounting, or social media management. Being resourceful is a key skill in the world of entrepreneurship.

Remember, a successful business doesn't require a massive initial investment. With a little creativity and resourcefulness, you can find ways to finance your teenage dream and turn your idea into a reality.

Building Your Teenage Dream Team (Optional):

This section is particularly relevant if you envision your business growing beyond a solo operation. Here are some tips for assembling a talented team:

- **Friends and Family:** Surround yourself with supportive friends and family members who share your passion and vision. Delegate tasks based on their strengths and interests.
- **Partnerships:** Consider collaborating with other teenagers who possess complementary skills or share resources. Look for individuals who can contribute different perspectives and expertise to your business.
- **Mentorship:** Seek guidance from experienced entrepreneurs or business professionals. A mentor can offer valuable advice and support throughout your entrepreneurial journey.

Remember, building a strong team can significantly enhance your business's growth potential. However, if you're starting solo, don't feel discouraged! Many successful businesses have been launched by a single passionate individual.

Embrace the Power of Planning: Setting Yourself Up for Success

Taking the time to plan your business venture may seem tedious, but it's a crucial investment that will pay off in the long run. A well-defined business plan becomes your roadmap to success, helping you stay focused, make informed decisions, and overcome challenges that might arise. With the tools and strategies outlined in this chapter, you're well on your way to turning your business idea into a thriving reality.

The Power of "No": Prioritizing and Saying Goodbye to Distractions

As a teenager, you juggle a lot: schoolwork, extracurricular activities, social life, and now, your burgeoning business. While passion and dedication are essential, effective time management is crucial for entrepreneurial success.

Here's a crucial lesson to learn early on: the power of "no." You won't be able to do everything, and that's okay! Learn to identify tasks that are less important or don't directly contribute to your business goals.

Here are some tips for prioritizing and saying goodbye to distractions:

- **Create a Schedule:** Develop a realistic schedule that allocates time for your business alongside your other commitments. Blocking time slots for specific tasks helps you stay focused and avoid procrastination.
- **Learn to Delegate:** If you have a team, delegate tasks whenever possible. This frees up your time to focus on the critical aspects of running your business and allows others to develop their skills.

- **Minimize Time-Sinks:** Social media, video games, and endless texting can easily devour your time. Set boundaries and limit your indulgence in these activities, especially during dedicated work hours.
- **Embrace the Pomodoro Technique:** This time management method involves working in focused 25-minute intervals with short breaks in between. This can help you maintain concentration and avoid burnout.
- **Just Say No:** Don't be afraid to politely decline requests that eat into your valuable business time. Remember, it's okay to prioritize your goals and say no to activities that don't align with your entrepreneurial journey.

Building a Strong Support System: Your Network is Your Net Worth

As a young entrepreneur, you don't have to navigate the business world alone. Building a strong support system is crucial for your success. Here's how to create your personal network:

- **Family and Friends:** Surround yourself with supportive people who believe in your dream. Share your ideas, seek their feedback, and leverage their connections if possible.
- **Mentors:** Find a mentor, an experienced entrepreneur or business professional who can offer guidance and answer your questions. Many organizations offer mentorship programs specifically for young entrepreneurs.
- **Online Communities:** Join online communities and forums for young entrepreneurs. Connect with like-minded individuals, share experiences, and learn from each other's successes and challenges.
- **Attend Events:** Look for workshops, conferences, or networking events designed for young entrepreneurs. These events offer valuable learning opportunities and a chance to connect with potential mentors, investors, or even future business partners.

Remember, your network is your net worth. The connections you build can provide invaluable support, resources, and opportunities as your business grows.

Embrace the Rollercoaster: Planning for Challenges and Setbacks

The road to entrepreneurial success is rarely smooth. Challenges and setbacks are inevitable. The key is to be prepared and resilient. Here are some tips for navigating the inevitable bumps along the way:

- **Expect the Unexpected:** Anticipate potential challenges by considering "what-if" scenarios. Having a backup plan can help you adapt and minimize the impact of unexpected hurdles.
- **Stay Positive:** Don't let setbacks discourage you. Maintain a positive attitude and view challenges as opportunities to learn and grow.
- **Celebrate Small Wins:** Take the time to acknowledge your progress, no matter how small. Celebrating these milestones can keep you motivated and focused on your long-term goals.
- **Learn from Mistakes:** Everyone makes mistakes, especially when starting a new venture. Analyze your missteps, learn from them, and adapt your approach for future success.
- **Seek Help When Needed:** Don't be afraid to ask for help when you need it. Reach out to your network of mentors, peers, or even online communities for advice and support.

Remember, the most successful entrepreneurs are the ones who can learn from their mistakes and bounce back from setbacks. Embrace the challenges, and you'll emerge from them stronger and more prepared to lead your business to new heights.

By following the strategies outlined in this chapter, you've laid the groundwork for a successful entrepreneurial adventure. You've identified your business idea, set clear goals, and developed a plan to navigate the exciting journey ahead. Now, let's dive into the world of launching your business! In the next chapter, we'll explore the art of creating a captivating brand identity, establishing a strong online presence, and implementing effective marketing strategies to reach your target audience.

Chapter IV: Launching Your Business - Take Off Like a Teenage Tycoon!

Congratulations! You've invested the time and effort to plan your dream business. Now, it's time to unleash your inner entrepreneur and launch your venture into the world. This chapter will equip you with the essential tools to create a captivating brand identity, establish a strong online presence, and attract a swarm of excited customers – all without needing a fancy degree or a corporate bank account!

Crafting Your Brand Identity: Be Unique, Be You!

Your brand identity is like your business's fingerprint. It's what sets you apart from the competition and tells your target audience who you are and what you stand for. Here's how to build a brand identity that resonates with your teenage customers:

- **Brainstorming Bonanza:** Grab your friends, some colorful markers, and get creative! Brainstorm words, phrases, and visuals that represent your brand's personality. What are your core values? What emotions do you want your brand to evoke?
- **The Power of a Name:** Choosing the right name for your business is crucial. It should be catchy, memorable, and easy to pronounce. Run your shortlisted names by your target audience to see what resonates with them.
- **Logo Love:** Your logo is a visual representation of your brand. It should be simple, eye-catching, and consistent with your overall brand identity. There are many free online logo design tools available for teenagers to explore.
- **Color Crush:** Colors evoke emotions and can influence customer perception. Choose a color palette that reflects your brand personality. For example, bright

and bold colors might represent a fun and energetic brand, while calming blues and greens might be a good fit for a wellness-focused business.
- **Social Media Savvy:** Since most teenagers are glued to their phones, social media is a fantastic platform to showcase your brand. Create engaging content that reflects your brand voice and personality. This could include product photos, behind-the-scenes glimpses, or even fun polls and quizzes.

Remember, your brand identity is a work in progress. It can evolve as your business grows, but the core values and personality you establish at the launch will resonate with your target audience and build brand loyalty.

Building Your Online Empire: Owning the Digital Space

In today's digital world, having a strong online presence is essential. Here are some ways teenagers can create a website or online store without needing a coding degree:

- **Website Wonders:** Many platforms offer user-friendly website building tools specifically designed for beginners. These platforms come with pre-designed templates and drag-and-drop functionality, allowing you to create a professional-looking website without any coding knowledge.
- **The Power of "Free":** There are many free website hosting services available. Explore these options to find a plan that suits your needs and budget.
- **E-commerce Essentials:** If you're selling products online, look for platforms that offer easy-to-use e-commerce functionalities. These platforms allow you to manage your inventory, process payments securely, and even offer features like discount codes and shipping options.
- **Content is King (and Queen!):** Fill your website with engaging content that informs and excites your target audience. This could include product descriptions, blog posts about your niche, or even tutorials related to your products or services.

- **Social Media Synergy:** Link your website to your social media accounts and vice versa. This drives traffic to your website and allows customers to learn more about your brand through multiple channels.

Remember, your website is your online storefront. Make it visually appealing, easy to navigate, and packed with information that compels customers to buy from you.

Marketing on a Budget: Spreading the Word Without Breaking the Bank

Marketing doesn't have to involve expensive advertising campaigns. Here are some creative and cost-effective ways to reach your target audience as a teenager:

- **Social Media Mastery:** Leverage the power of social media platforms like Instagram, TikTok, or YouTube. Create engaging content that showcases your products or services, and participate in relevant online communities to connect with potential customers.
- **Word-of-Mouth Magic:** One of the most powerful marketing tools is free! Tell your friends, family, and classmates about your business. Encourage them to spread the word and share their positive experiences with others.
- **Local Love:** Get involved in your local community. Participate in craft fairs, farmers markets, or school events to showcase your products and connect with potential customers face-to-face.
- **Collaboration is Key:** Partner with other young entrepreneurs or local businesses to cross-promote each other's products or services. This allows you to reach a wider audience without a significant investment.
- **Content Marketing Marvel:** Create valuable content that educates and entertains your target audience, without directly promoting your product or service. This could involve:
    - **Blog Posts:** Share your knowledge and expertise related to your niche. Write informative blog posts about topics that your target audience is interested in. For example, if you sell handmade jewelry, you could write

blog posts about different jewelry-making techniques or interesting facts about gemstones.
- **DIY Videos:** Create engaging video tutorials demonstrating how to use your product or service. This is a fantastic way to showcase the value you offer and attract potential customers.
- **Social Media Stories & Reels:** Utilize platforms like Instagram Stories or TikTok Reels to share behind-the-scenes glimpses of your business, product creation process, or even fun challenges related to your niche. Short, engaging videos are a great way to grab attention and build brand awareness.
- **Collaborations with Influencers:** Partner with teenage influencers who share your target audience. This could involve creating a sponsored post or video where they showcase your product or service to their followers. Remember, choose influencers who align with your brand values and whose audience genuinely resonates with your offerings.

- **Remember, consistency is key! Regularly creating engaging content keeps your brand at the forefront of your audience's mind and establishes you as an authority in your niche.**

Customer Service Superstar: Building Loyalty That Lasts

Providing excellent customer service is crucial for building brand loyalty and encouraging repeat business. Here are some tips for teenagers to shine as customer service superstars:

- **Be Responsive:** Respond to customer inquiries and messages promptly and professionally. This shows your customers that you value their business and are dedicated to their satisfaction.
- **Go the Extra Mile:** Small gestures can go a long way. Include a handwritten thank you note with orders, offer personalized

recommendations, or even throw in a free sample with a purchase. These little surprises can delight your customers and make them feel valued.
- **Embrace Feedback:** Welcome customer feedback, both positive and negative. Use it to improve your products, services, and overall customer experience.
- **Be Authentic:** Let your personality shine through in your interactions with customers. Be friendly, helpful, and genuinely interested in their needs. Customers connect with authenticity, and it helps build trust and loyalty.

- **Remember, happy customers are your best marketing tool. By providing exceptional customer service, you'll not only retain existing customers but also encourage them to sing your praises to their friends and family.**
Launching Your Business: The Big Day (and Beyond!)
The day you officially launch your business is a cause for celebration! But remember, this is just the beginning of your entrepreneurial journey. Here are some final tips to ensure a successful launch and set yourself up for long-term growth:
    - **Pre-Launch Hype:** Create a buzz around your launch! Announce your business on social media, run a contest or giveaway to generate excitement, and offer special launch discounts to attract early adopters.
    - **Soft Launch Option:** Consider a soft launch to a limited audience (friends, family, classmates) before opening your doors (or online store) to the public. This allows you to gather feedback and iron out any kinks before a full-fledged launch.

- **Embrace the Learning Curve:** There will be bumps along the road. Don't be afraid to experiment, adapt your strategies, and learn from your experiences.
- **Celebrate Your Wins:** Take time to acknowledge your achievements, big and small. Celebrating your successes keeps you motivated and reminds you of how far you've come.
- **Keep Learning:** The world of business is constantly evolving. Stay up-to-date on industry trends, attend workshops or webinars, and connect with other young entrepreneurs to keep learning and growing.

- **Launching your business as a teenager is an exciting and empowering adventure. By following the strategies outlined in this chapter, you have the tools and knowledge to navigate the exciting world of entrepreneurship. So, take a deep breath, unleash your inner business whiz, and get ready to launch your teenage empire!**

Here are some strategies a young person in Africa with no internet access can use to start a business:

1. Identify Local Needs and Resources:

- **Talk to People:** Chat with friends, family, and neighbors to understand what products or services are lacking in their community.exclamation Is there something people need that isn't readily available?
- **Observe Your Surroundings:** Look for problems or inefficiencies in your community. Is there a product people have to travel far to buy? Could a service be made more convenient?
- **Consider Local Resources:** What skills or resources are readily available in your community? Are there natural materials that can be used to create products? Are there people with specific skills you can partner with?

2. Leverage Traditional Communication Channels:

- **Spread the Word:** Once you have an idea, tell everyone you know! Talk to friends, family, and local shopkeepers about your product or service. Word-of-mouth marketing is powerful, especially in close-knit communities.expand_more
- **Get Creative with Marketing:** Think beyond traditional advertising. Create eye-catching flyers or posters to display in local shops or community centers. Even a simple chalkboard outside your home can advertise your business.

3. Build Relationships and Collaborate:

- **Partner with Local Businesses:** Approach shopkeepers or vendors in your area and see if they'd be interested in selling your products. You could offer them a commission on each sale.
- **Find a Mentor:** Talk to experienced business owners in your community. They might be willing to offer guidance and support, even if it's just sharing their knowledge and experience.
- **Barter System:** Explore bartering your goods or services for things you need. For example, if you fix someone's bicycle, they might offer you fresh produce in exchange.

4. Focus on Providing Excellent Customer Service:

- **Build Trust:** Since you won't have online reviews, focus on building trust with your customers through excellent service. Be reliable, friendly, and always deliver on your promises.
- **Go the Extra Mile:** Small gestures can make a big difference. Offer free repairs, throw in a small gift with a purchase, or simply remember your customers' preferences. This kind of personalized service will keep people coming back for more.
- **Get Feedback and Adapt:** Talk to your customers and ask for their feedback. What are they happy with? What can you improve? Use their feedback to constantly refine your product or service and better meet their needs.
- Remember, even without internet access, there are plenty of ways for a young person in Africa to start a successful business. By focusing on local needs, leveraging traditional communication channels, building relationships, and providing excellent customer service, you can turn your entrepreneurial dream into a reality.

Here are the key takeaways from Chapter IV:

- **Brand Identity is Key:** Craft a unique and memorable brand identity that resonates with your target audience.
- **Embrace the Digital Space (if possible):** Build a user-friendly website or online store to showcase your products or services. Utilize social media platforms to connect with customers and promote your brand.
- **Marketing on a Budget:** Get creative with marketing strategies that don't require a big budget. Leverage social media, word-of-mouth marketing, local events, and collaborations with other young entrepreneurs.
- **Content is King:** Create informative and engaging content that educates and entertains your target audience, establishing you as an authority in your niche.
- **Customer Service Superstar:** Provide exceptional customer service to build brand loyalty and encourage repeat business. Be responsive, go the extra mile, and value customer feedback.
- **Celebrate Your Wins and Keep Learning:** Acknowledge your achievements, big and small. Stay updated on industry trends, and continuously learn and adapt to ensure long-term growth.

Bonus takeaway (applicable to those without internet access):

- **Focus on Local Needs:** Identify problems or unmet needs within your community and tailor your business idea to address them.
- **Traditional Marketing Power:** Utilize word-of-mouth marketing, flyers, and creative signage to spread the word about your business.
- **Build Relationships:** Collaborate with local businesses, find mentors, and explore barter systems to expand your reach and resources.

Chapter V: Running Your Business Like a Pro - From Teenage Tycoon to Young Enterprise Mogul!

Congratulations, superstar entrepreneur! You've launched your business, and the world is your oyster. But hold on tight, because the rollercoaster ride of running a successful business is just beginning. This chapter equips you with the tools and inspiration to navigate the exciting – and sometimes challenging – journey of transforming your teenage dream into a thriving enterprise. Buckle up, because we're about to show you how to run your business like a seasoned pro!

From Lemonade Stands to Million-Dollar Empires: Real-World Inspiration

Before diving into strategies, let's get a dose of inspiration! Remember lemonade stands? Sure, they were adorable, but they were also the training grounds for some of today's youngest business moguls. Take Mikaila Ulmer, for example. This phenomenal teenager, at the tender age of 10, started a business selling her own bee sting lemonade recipe – "Bee Sweet Lemonade" – to raise awareness about the declining bee population. Her passion and initiative not only landed her a spot on "Shark Tank" but also sparked a national conversation about environmental sustainability.

There's also Harvey Karp, the creator of the revolutionary "Happiest Baby on the Block" white noise machine. Do you know when he got the idea? At 21 years old, while desperately trying to soothe his colicky daughter! His determination to find a solution not only helped countless parents around the world but also turned into a multi-million dollar business.

These are just a few examples of young people who dared to dream big and turned their ideas into reality. They're a living testament to the fact that age is just a number when it comes to entrepreneurial success. Now, let's explore the secrets they (unconsciously) followed to become business rockstars!

Mastering the Money Game: Budgeting Like a Boss

Money makes the business world go round, but managing it effectively can feel like a high-stakes juggling act. Don't worry, we've got you covered!

- **Track Every Penny:** Develop a system for recording your income and expenses – a simple notebook works wonders! Knowing where your money goes is crucial for making informed financial decisions.
- **Budgeting is Your BFF:** Create a budget that allocates your funds towards essential business needs like materials, marketing, and even saving for future investments.
- **Separate Your Piggy Banks:** Keep your personal finances separate from your business finances. This helps maintain clarity and avoids unnecessary spending.

Remember, financial responsibility is a superpower for young entrepreneurs! By managing your money wisely, you'll lay the foundation for long-term business growth.

The Customer is King (or Queen): Building Customer Loyalty

In the business world, happy customers are your golden ticket to success. Here's how to make them feel like royalty:

- **Deliver Stellar Service:** Be responsive, friendly, and always go the extra mile to fulfill customer needs. A positive customer experience keeps people coming back for more and singing your praises to their friends.
- **The Power of Feedback:** Actively seek customer feedback, both positive and negative. Use it to improve your products, services, and overall customer experience.

- **Reward Loyalty:** Show your appreciation for repeat customers with special offers, discounts, or even a simple handwritten thank you note. These small gestures build loyalty and make them feel valued.

Remember, happy customers are your biggest cheerleaders! By prioritizing their needs and exceeding expectations, you'll cultivate a loyal customer base that fuels your business success.

The Art of the Deal: Mastering Negotiation Skills

Negotiation might sound intimidating, but it's a crucial skill for young entrepreneurs. Here are some tips to sharpen your negotiation game:

- **Do Your Research:** Knowledge is power! Before any negotiation, research the market value of products or services involved. This equips you to make informed decisions and avoid getting ripped off.
- **Confidence is Key:** Project confidence even if you're feeling nervous. Speak clearly, state your value proposition clearly, and be prepared to walk away if the deal doesn't meet your needs.
- **Win-Win Mentality:** Aim for a win-win situation in every negotiation. Focus on finding common ground and creating a mutually beneficial agreement.

Remember, negotiation is a conversation, not a battle. By being prepared, confident, and fair, you'll strike deals that benefit your business and leave everyone happy.

Growth is the Goal: Taking Your Business to the Next Level

Your business is your baby, and you want it to thrive! Here are some strategies to propel your venture towards exciting new heights:

- **Expand Your Offerings:** As your business grows, consider adding new products or services that complement your existing offerings.

Real-World Inspiration.

There's also Harvey Karp, the creator of the revolutionary "Happiest Baby on the Block" white noise machine. Do you know when he got the idea? At 21 years old, while desperately trying to soothe his colicky daughter! His determination to find a solution not only helped countless parents around the world but also turned into a multi-million dollar business.

These are just a few examples of young people who dared to dream big and turned their ideas into reality. They're a living testament to the fact that age is just a number when it comes to entrepreneurial success. Now, let's explore the secrets they (unconsciously) followed to become business rockstars!

Beyond Lemonade Stands: A Broader Look at Young Business Leaders

The world of young entrepreneurs is brimming with inspiring stories. Here are a few more examples to ignite your entrepreneurial spirit:

- **David Karp (Tumblr):** At just 19 years old, David Karp co-founded Tumblr, a microblogging platform that revolutionized social media by allowing users to share multimedia content with ease. Tumblr's innovative approach and focus on user experience propelled it to become a social media giant, eventually being acquired by Yahoo for a whopping $1.1 billion!
- **Nick D'Aloisio (Summly):** This teenage prodigy developed Summly, an app that summarized news articles using artificial intelligence, at the ripe old age of 15. His groundbreaking idea caught the eye of tech giant Yahoo, who acquired

Summly for a reported $30 million, making Nick the youngest person ever to have a company acquired for such a high value.
- **Belal Khan (WeFarm):** Belal Khan's story is one of social impact and agricultural innovation. At 17, he co-founded WeFarm, a mobile platform that connects small-scale farmers in Africa with essential information, resources, and market opportunities. WeFarm empowers farmers to increase their yields, improve their livelihoods, and contribute to a more sustainable food system.

These young leaders come from diverse backgrounds and tackled different challenges, but their stories share a common thread – passion, innovation, and a relentless drive to make a difference. They prove that anyone, regardless of age, can become a successful entrepreneur with the right idea and the willingness to work hard.

Remember, you are surrounded by potential! Look around you, identify a problem, and brainstorm solutions. The next big business idea could be brewing right in your mind, waiting to be unleashed and transform the world!

Chapter VI: Growing Your Business - From Budding Sprout to Thriving Redwood!

Hey there, young entrepreneur extraordinaire! You've launched your business, weathered the initial storms, and are now ready to witness it blossom into something truly remarkable. This chapter is your guide to nurturing your business from a tender seedling into a towering redwood, a symbol of strength, resilience, and lasting success. Here's the exciting part: growth isn't just about numbers; it's about watching your dream take root, branch out, and provide shade and inspiration for others!

Fanning the Flames of Innovation: Keeping Your Ideas Fresh

The world of business thrives on fresh ideas. Here's how to keep your creative juices flowing:

- **Embrace Curiosity:** Cultivate a curious mind! Ask questions, explore new things, and stay up-to-date on industry trends. Innovation often sparks from unexpected places, so be open to inspiration wherever it strikes.
- **Befriend Brainstorming:** Gather your friends, family, or even fellow young entrepreneurs and brainstorm new ideas. Bounce ideas off each other, challenge assumptions, and see where your collective creativity takes you.
- **Embrace Feedback:** Don't be afraid of constructive criticism! Feedback from customers, mentors, and even competitors can reveal blind spots and ignite new possibilities for growth.

Remember, innovation is the lifeblood of any thriving business. By staying curious, fostering collaboration, and welcoming feedback, you'll ensure your business stays at the forefront and continues to excite your customers.

Building Your Dream Team: The Power of Collaboration

You might be a one-person powerhouse right now, but as your business grows, consider assembling a dream team. Here's why:

- **Strength in Numbers:** Surrounding yourself with talented individuals with complementary skills allows you to tackle bigger challenges and achieve more significant goals.
- **Diverse Perspectives:** A team with diverse backgrounds and experiences brings fresh ideas and solutions to the table, fostering innovation and growth.
- **Shared Passion:** Building a team of people who share your passion for your mission creates a supportive and dynamic environment where everyone feels empowered to contribute their best.

Remember, collaboration isn't just about delegating tasks; it's about harnessing the collective power of brilliant minds. Seek out individuals who inspire you, share your vision, and are excited to embark on this entrepreneurial adventure together.

Marketing Magic: Reaching New Heights with Your Brand

As your business expands, so should your reach. Here are some strategies to get your brand in front of a wider audience:

- **Level Up Your Online Presence:** Consider investing in professional website design or explore advanced functionalities of your e-commerce platform to enhance user experience.
- **Social Media Savvy:** Experiment with new social media platforms and tailor your content to each one. Utilize paid advertising options to target specific demographics or reach a wider audience.
- **Content is King (and Queen!):** Develop a content strategy that goes beyond just promoting your products or services. Create informative articles, host engaging webinars, or even launch a podcast to establish yourself as an authority in your niche.
- **Think Outside the Box:** Explore creative marketing opportunities! Partner with local businesses, participate in relevant events, or even launch a social media challenge to generate buzz and excitement around your brand.

Remember, reaching new customers is about building relationships and showcasing the value you offer. Experiment, find what resonates with your target audience, and watch your brand recognition soar!

Giving Back: The Power of Purpose

Remember, a successful business isn't just about financial gain. It's about making a positive impact on the world. Here are some ways to integrate purpose into your company culture:

- **Embrace Sustainability:** Look for ways to reduce your environmental footprint or support eco-friendly practices.
- **Give Back to the Community:** Partner with local charities or causes you care about. Organize volunteer events, donate a portion of your profits, or use your platform to raise awareness for important issues.
- **Empower Others:** Share your entrepreneurial journey with other young people. Offer mentorship opportunities, host workshops, or simply inspire them to believe in their own dreams.

Remember, success is sweeter when shared. By integrating social responsibility into your business model, you create a legacy that extends far beyond the bottom line.

Growing Your Business is Growing You!

The journey of growing your business is an incredible adventure filled with challenges, triumphs, and endless learning opportunities. Embrace the process, celebrate your victories, and never stop learning and adapting. Remember, you are on the path to becoming not just a successful entrepreneur, but a powerful force for positive change in the world. So, keep dreaming big, keep innovating, and keep growing that business like the magnificent redwood it's destined to be! The world is waiting.

This chapter is a great start! Here's some expert advice to make it even more impactful for young entrepreneurs:

Fanning the Flames of Innovation:

- **Embrace Constraints:** Sometimes limitations breed creativity. Challenge yourself to solve problems with limited resources or a tight timeframe. This can lead to innovative and cost-effective solutions.
- **Learn from Others (But Don't Copy):** Research what established businesses in your industry are doing, but don't simply imitate them. Find inspiration in their strategies and adapt them to fit your unique brand and target audience.
- **Step Outside Your Comfort Zone:** Attend industry conferences, workshops, or online courses to expose yourself to new ideas and technologies. Talk to experts in different fields – you never know where the next spark of inspiration might come from.

Building Your Dream Team:

- **Start Small, Scale Smart:** You don't need a massive team from the get-go. Identify the most critical roles to support your immediate growth and recruit individuals with those specific skillsets. As your business expands, you can strategically add more team members.
- **Invest in Training and Development:** Empower your team by providing them with opportunities to learn and grow. This could involve online courses, mentorship programs, or even sending them to industry events. A well-trained and motivated team is your greatest asset.
- **Foster a Culture of Collaboration:** Encourage open communication and teamwork within your company. Create a safe space where team members feel comfortable sharing ideas, offering constructive criticism, and learning from each other.

Marketing Magic:

- **Data-Driven Decisions:** Don't just throw marketing spaghetti at the wall and see what sticks! Track your marketing campaigns using analytics tools. Analyze the data to see what's working and what's not. This allows you to optimize your strategies and maximize your return on investment (ROI).
- **Micro-Influencers:** Consider partnering with micro-influencers – social media personalities with a smaller but highly engaged following – to promote your brand. They can often connect with your target audience on a more personal level than larger influencers.
- **Build an Email List:** Email marketing remains a powerful tool for reaching your target audience directly. Create valuable and engaging email content to nurture leads, convert sales, and build long-term customer relationships.

Giving Back: The Power of Purpose

- **Find a Cause You Care About:** Don't just support random charities. Choose a cause that aligns with your brand values and resonates with your team and target audience. This will create a more authentic and impactful social impact initiative.
- **Get Your Customers Involved:** Encourage your customers to join your social responsibility efforts. Organize fundraising campaigns, offer eco-friendly product options, or allow customers to donate a portion of their purchase to charity.
- **Measure Your Impact:** Track the impact of your social responsibility initiatives. This could involve quantifiable metrics like the amount of money raised or trees planted, or qualitative data like customer feedback and employee engagement.

Growing Your Business is Growing You!

- **Develop a Growth Mindset:** Believe that you and your business can learn and improve. Embrace challenges as opportunities to grow and don't be afraid to step outside your comfort zone.
- **Find a Mentor:** Connect with a successful entrepreneur or business professional who can offer guidance and support. A mentor can share valuable insights, help you avoid common pitfalls, and celebrate your successes with you.
- **Never Stop Learning:** The world of business is constantly evolving. Stay up-to-date on industry trends, read business publications, and attend relevant workshops or conferences. The more you learn, the better equipped you'll be to navigate the challenges and opportunities that lie ahead.

By incorporating these expert tips, you can transform Chapter VI into a comprehensive guide that empowers young entrepreneurs to not only grow their businesses but also become well-rounded, innovative, and socially responsible leaders.

Key Takeaways from Your Entrepreneurial Journey:

- **You Have the Power:** Age is just a number. You possess the passion, creativity, and drive to become a successful entrepreneur.
- **Embrace Lifelong Learning:** The business world is constantly evolving. Stay curious, seek out knowledge, and never stop learning.
- **Building a Brand You Love:** Craft a unique brand identity that resonates with your target audience and reflects your values.
- **The Power of Strategy:** Develop practical strategies for marketing, budgeting, customer service, and negotiation to ensure your business thrives.

- **Innovation is Key:** Stay curious, explore new ideas, and embrace feedback to fuel continuous innovation in your business.
- **Assemble Your Dream Team:** Surround yourself with talented individuals who share your vision and complement your skillset.
- **Marketing Magic:** Reach new customers and build brand awareness through targeted online marketing strategies and creative community engagement.
- **Giving Back is Rewarding:** Integrate social responsibility into your business model to create a positive impact on the world.
- **Embrace Challenges:** Setbacks are inevitable, but they are also valuable learning opportunities. Analyze mistakes, adapt, and keep moving forward with determination.
- **Dream Big, Always:** Don't be limited by your circumstances. Set ambitious goals, unleash your creativity, and believe in your ability to achieve greatness.
- **The Future is Yours:** Young entrepreneurs are the driving force behind innovation and positive change in the business world. Use your voice, leverage technology, and make a difference.

Remember, you are not just building a business; you are building a legacy. So, go forth, young entrepreneur, and conquer your dreams!